EXPLORING THE SCIENCE OF NATURE

# The Nature and Science of
# SPRING

## Jane Burton and Kim Taylor

Gareth Stevens Publishing
**MILWAUKEE**

For a free color catalog describing Gareth Stevens Publishing's list of high-quality books
and multimedia programs, call 1-800-542-2595 (USA) or 1-800-461-9120 (Canada).
Gareth Stevens Publishing's Fax: (414) 225-0377.

**Library of Congress Cataloging-in-Publication Data**

Burton, Jane.
The nature and science of spring / by Jane Burton and Kim Taylor.
p. cm. — (Exploring the science of nature)
Includes bibliographical references and index.
Summary: Explains why the season of spring happens and how it
manifests itself in the weather and changes in plants and animals.
ISBN 0-8368-2188-2 (lib. bdg.)
1. Spring—Juvenile literature. [1. Spring.] I. Taylor, Kim.
II. Title. III. Series: Burton, Jane.
Exploring the science of nature.
QB637.5.B87    1999
508.2—dc21        99-29593

First published in North America in 1999 by
**Gareth Stevens Publishing**
1555 North RiverCenter Drive, Suite 201
Milwaukee, Wisconsin 53212 USA

This U.S. edition © 1999 by Gareth Stevens, Inc. Created with original © 1999 by
White Cottage Children's Books. Text © 1999 by Kim Taylor. Photographs © 1999 by
Jane Burton, Kim Taylor, and Mark Taylor. The photographs on pages 22 (*above*) and
27 (*above*) are by Jan Taylor. Conceived, designed, and produced by White Cottage
Children's Books, 29 Lancaster Park, Richmond, Surrey TW10 6AB, England.
Additional end matter © 1999 by Gareth Stevens, Inc.

The rights of Jane Burton and Kim Taylor to be identified as the authors of this work
have been asserted by them in accordance with the Copyright, Design and Patents
Act 1988. Educational consultant, Jane Weaver; scientific adviser, Dr. Jan Taylor.

Printed in the United States of America

1 2 3 4 5 6 7 8 9 03 02 01 00 99

# Contents

Words that appear in the glossary are printed in **boldface** type the first time they occur in the text.

# The Meaning of Spring

The change of seasons is caused by the changing position of Earth in relation to the Sun. Some scientists believe the seasons were first caused by an event that took place a very long time ago. At that time, Earth was a huge blob of molten rock and metal, traveling in an orbit around the Sun. Earth was straight up and down, spinning on an imaginary **axis**. Days on the red-hot Earth were always the same length. There were no seasons.

During this same time, there was also another, smaller blob of molten rock and metal traveling around the Sun. Some scientists believe that the smaller blob smashed into Earth with such force that it knocked Earth's axis 23 degrees away from its upright position, and the axis has been tilted ever since. This change in the position of Earth's axis resulted in different seasons.

During spring in the Northern **Hemisphere**, Earth is at a point in its orbit when the northern end of its axis is beginning to point more toward the Sun. With each passing day, the Sun climbs higher in the sky, and **day length** increases. At the same time, the southern end of Earth's axis points more away from the Sun, and it is autumn in the Southern Hemisphere.

The spring **equinox** occurs on March 20 or 21 in the Northern Hemisphere.

**Above:** The European jay lines its nest with materials like this tiny tree root.

**Top:** A budding twig from a goat willow tree announces spring.

**Opposite:** In spring, a sea of bluebells spreads beneath the trees in a European woods. A pheasant surveys its beautiful domain.

**Below:** A young gray squirrel looks around inquisitively among the wood anemones.

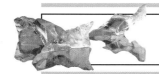

# Melting Ice

**Top and below:**
Melting ice is sculpted into unusual shapes.

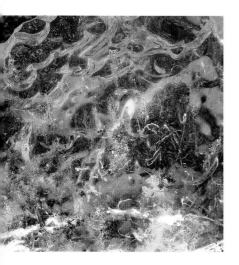

A block of ice does not melt as soon as it is warmed above the freezing point of water at 32° Fahrenheit (0° Celsius). It can stay at the freezing point for some time before it starts to melt. The ice soaks up warmth and gradually begins to drip. The temperature of the drips is 32°F (0°C). The ice takes in heat, but its temperature does not rise. The heat required to melt a solid is called its **latent heat**. The latent heat of ice is much greater than that of many other solids, for example, candle wax.

It is good that ice melts slowly. Otherwise, the spring thaw could have disastrous effects each year.

**Right:** The long days of spring in the Arctic are warm enough to make chunks of ice break away from glaciers. The chunks are called icebergs.

**Left:** Some waterfalls, such as this one in Yosemite National Park in California, flow spectacularly only in spring when snow melts on the mountains above.

**Below:** Glacier lily buds push up through the snow. When the snow melts, the flowers open, ready for the first insects to visit.

If there were no such thing as latent heat, snow and ice would melt suddenly, all at one time, producing catastrophic floods.

Because ice melts slowly, plants and animals have time to **adapt** to the gradual changes brought by the spring thaw. Plants living beneath the snow sense the rise in temperature in spring. Their roots become surrounded by wet soil, not frozen soil, and the plants start to grow.

Many kinds of plants that spend the winter as **bulbs** send up flowers that burst out through the snow in early spring. These plants have a head start over other kinds of plants that do not begin to grow until after the snow melts.

# Lengthening Days

**Top:** A young adder basks in the warm sunshine of spring.

**Above:** Flies, including a large bluebottle fly, huddle together for warmth in the early spring sunshine.

**Right:** A European rabbit fluffs up its fur to make the most of the Sun's warmth.

When the spring equinox occurs anywhere in the world, day and night are each twelve hours long. Following the spring equinox, days get longer, and nights become shorter.

Each morning following the spring equinox, the Sun rises earlier. Each evening, it sets later. The farther away from the Equator, the longer each day becomes in relation to the previous day. During spring in polar regions, today's day length may be several minutes longer than yesterday's.

As spring advances, the Sun climbs higher in the sky. Its rays pass through much less of Earth's atmosphere, which means that more of the Sun's heat and light strike the actual ground. Spring sunshine is warm and comforting, and animals emerge from **hibernation** to bask in it.

Basking in the Sun's warmth is the only way that many **cold-blooded** animals can raise their body temperature. They need to warm up before their muscles will work properly. Butterflies bask on flat surfaces facing the Sun. They position their wings to catch as much of the warmth as possible. Flies may get some protection from an unwelcome breeze by clustering together while basking. Lizards bask alone, ready to dart for cover at the first sign of danger.

**Above:** Butterflies bask in different ways. The painted lady spreads its wings flat to soak up as much of the Sun as possible.

Even mammals, which are **warm-blooded**, sometimes bask in the Sun. They enjoy the warmth and use the Sun's **ultraviolet rays** to produce vitamin D in the oil on their skin. They ingest the oil when they lick their fur. In that way, they replace the vitamin D that was used up during the dark winter months.

**Above:** A wall brown butterfly holds its wings in such a way to reflect the Sun's rays onto its body.

**Right:** A brimstone butterfly does not open its wings to bask. Instead, it tilts its body over so that its underside catches the Sun's rays.

# Spring Rains

**Top:** Giant spider mites with coats of rich red velvet creep over the ground at the start of the African rainy season.

**Above:** Giant millipedes sometimes appear by the hundreds at the start of the rainy season in warm countries. They reach almost 6 inches (15 centimeters) in length.

**Right:** Zebras stand motionless as a rainstorm sweeps across the plains in Africa .

Many warm regions of the world do not have four seasons. Their seasons are related to rainfall — not to temperature. Dry seasons, when there is no rain, result in conditions much like winter in cold countries. During the dry season, plants cannot grow, and many shrivel and die. Animals are short of food.

The coming of the rainy season in these regions is like spring. In just a few days, brown, parched land becomes lush and green. Flowers bloom, and trees grow a crop of fresh green leaves.

The start of the rainy season is a time of great activity in the animal world. Giant millipedes leave their dry-season hiding places and glide over the ground, searching for mates. Brilliant red velvet mites also suddenly appear on the ground. The air may fill with thousands of winged termites.

Moths and butterflies that have spent the dry season as **pupae** hatch and start looking for fresh leaves on which to lay their eggs. Beetles emerge from their dry-season shelters and scurry busily around or zoom from tree to tree. Birds sing, and frogs croak at the start of the rains, just as they do in springtime in colder climates.

Most animals **breed** and rear their young during the rainy season because there is plenty of food available at this time.

**Above:** The ground in warm countries can contain numerous plant bulbs. These lilies waited until the start of the rainy season before bursting into flower.

**Above:** Lilies often attract beetles. The beetles may eat the flowers within a few hours of their opening.

11

# Bursting Buds

One of the first things to happen in spring is that trees start taking in water from the soil through their roots. The water transforms into a liquid called **sap**. Sap flows in the tree's **phloem** layer, which is just below the bark. It flows up the tree's trunk, out along its branches, through the twigs, and into the leaf buds. Some trees make so much sap that it bursts out from cracks in the bark and out from damaged twigs.

Leaf buds, located on the ends of twigs during long winter months, begin to swell as sap flows into them. New leaves, folded and tightly packed inside the buds, are built of tiny cells with very little water in them. When the sap starts to flow, the cells fill with liquid and expand, causing the new leaves to burst out from the bud scales.

The fresh young leaves and the shoots on which they grow expand quickly. This is possible because all the cells are already formed. They just need to be pumped full of liquid. Each cell is like a balloon, waiting for something to pump it up.

Sap is not simply water. It contains sugar and minerals that are needed as food so that the cells in the leaves can multiply.

Cell multiplication is a slow process compared with expansion, however. The rate at which new leaves grow is much slower.

**Top:** A hazelnut tree has blossomed.

**Above:** New banksia leaves in spring in Australia are yellow. They turn green later.

**Opposite:** Beech leaves in spring are a pale green.

**Above:** Pieris leaves start out red. They later turn bronze and green.

**Below:** Brown bud scales flake off fresh green spruce needles.

# First Flowers

**Top:** Bullfinches munch on silvery pussy willow **catkins** in early spring.

**Above:** In spring, dangling yellow male alder catkins shed thousands of pollen grains into the breeze. The female flowers look like small purple cones.

**Right:** Crocuses spread their petals wide in the spring sunshine, so that honeybees can gather the pollen.

Many plants, including trees, flower in spring. Spring is the perfect season for plants to flower because this allows plenty of time for fruits and seeds to ripen during the warm weather of summer and autumn.

Flowers need to be **fertilized** before seeds can form. Insects and flowers need to work together to accomplish this in spring, each helping the other. Flowers produce bright colors and strong scents to attract insects. The insects carry **pollen** from one flower to another. The flowers reward the pollen-carrying insects with nourishing **nectar**.

Not all plants need insects to carry their pollen. Some trees produce catkins instead of flowers with colorful petals. Most catkins are designed to release pollen into the air so that the pollen drifts to other

**Left:** A magnolia tree becomes covered in showy, cup-shaped blossoms in early spring before the leaf buds open.

**Below:** Insects will soon be attracted to this flowering currant bush to feed on its nectar.

**Below:** Clusters of tiny lime-green flowers burst from the bud scales of a Norway maple.

flowers. The catkins of alder, birch, and hazel trees are small and hard during winter. In early spring, they grow rapidly and hang downward, shedding their yellow pollen into the wind.

The long, soft catkins are the open male flowers of these trees. Pine trees have similar male flowers, but they grow upward rather than hang down. The female flowers of these trees, which collect the pollen, are separate. They may not look like flowers at all. Trees that produce catkins do not have to rely on insects. Their flowers open in very early spring when the weather is still too cold for bees and other insects to be active.

15

 # Sleepers Awake

The first warm, sunny days of spring awaken insects that have spent the winter hibernating. Some of the first insects to visit spring flowers are the remarkable bee flies. They have round, furry bodies and are expert at hovering. A bee fly seems to hang motionless in front of a flower, like a miniature hummingbird, while it sips nectar with its long **proboscis**.

The butterfly **species** that hibernate as adults awaken in early spring. They fly around in sunshine, searching for early spring flowers on which to feed. If the day becomes cloudy, these butterflies quickly disappear. If the weather turns cold again, they may go back into hibernation. Later in spring, the butterfly species that hibernate as pupae appear. These species cannot go back into hibernation and need warm weather to survive.

**Right:** Honey stored in hanging combs keeps honeybees alive during winter. When the temperatures get warmer, worker bees leave the combs in search of spring flowers.

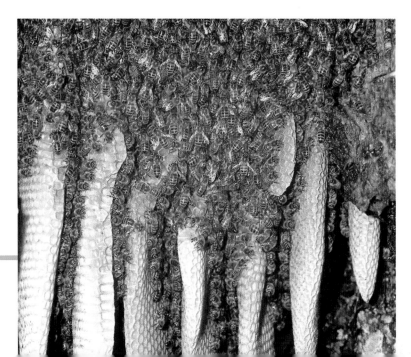

**Above:** A bee fly hovers in front of an honesty flower. The front legs and proboscis of the bee fly are smothered in pollen.

**Above:** At a flower, a bee fly's wings beat rapidly to support its weight. It rests its feet on the flower's petals as it feeds on nectar.

Queen wasps emerge from hibernation in early spring. They chew at the surface of wooden posts and fences to make wood pulp. The pulp is used to build a round paper nest that is 1-1½ inches (3-4 cm) across. In it, the queen rears her first **brood** of about ten workers.

Unlike wasp workers that all die in autumn, honeybee workers survive the winter. They keep themselves warm in winter by eating stored honey. As soon as the spring flowers start to open, the entire hive of workers is ready to fly from the hive to collect nectar.

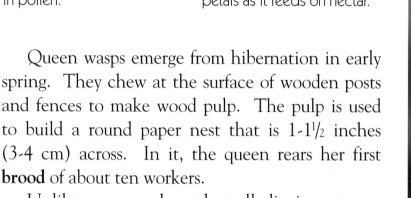

**Above:** A queen Saxony wasp molds a blob of wood pulp that she has collected to form the wall of her paper nest. The nest is attached to the hem of a curtain.

**Left:** A worker honeybee collects nectar from a spring squill flower.

**Top:** A common toad walks steadily on its spring journey to a pond.

**Above:** Stentors are tiny, trumpet-shaped, freshwater animals. Oxygen bubbles lifted these two types of stentors to the water's surface.

**Right:** With the warm-up in spring, the shallow margins of a lake teem with microscopic life.

Other signs of life appear in ponds and streams. In the warm spring sunshine, tiny green animals in the mud produce small bubbles of oxygen. As the bubbles grow, they rise to the surface, taking with them some of the mud and a host of **microscopic** life. This bubbly mud forms a scum on the surface of the pond where the water is warmest. It teems with life.

In spring, activity also begins among the small fishes. Male sticklebacks glow brilliant red around the gills, and their eyes turn turquoise. Their character also changes. Each male becomes fiercely **territorial**. Each has his own little area at the bottom of a pond, which he guards ferociously.

**Above:** By swimming forward with his tail and backward with his fins, a male stickleback is able to hover in front of his nest.

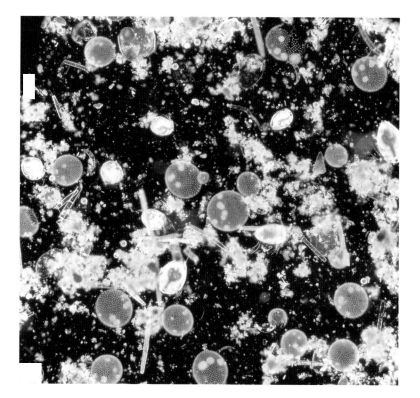

**Above:** Debris at the bottom of a pond contains a wealth of microscopic life. Here, round volvoxes drift among banana-shaped and long, green desmids. Two species of water fleas move around, stirring up the area.

**Above:** A female stickleback bulges with eggs. When a male notices her shape, he will not chase her away.

Each male stickleback builds a nest near the center of its territory out of pieces of water plants. The nest is a short tunnel that is open at both ends. At first, even female sticklebacks are chased away from the nest.

Females that are ready to lay eggs are bulgy. The males recognize this bulgy shape and become very interested. A male leads a bulgy female to the nest. Instead of being chased off, she is able to dive into the nest and lay her eggs. The male then fertilizes the eggs.

**Below:** The female stickleback enters the male's nest and lays her eggs. The male guards and cares for the eggs and the babies.

**Right:** A male common toad stops at coltsfoot flowers on his way to a **spawning** pond.

Spring is an exciting and dangerous time for toads. They live most of their lives on land. During winter, they hibernate in burrows or under logs. When spring comes, toads need to travel to water. Traveling at night, they scramble up banks, down ditches, through brambles, and across roads until they come to their well-known spawning places. These may be lakes or ponds where toads gather each spring by the hundreds. The males make croaking sounds.

Spring, or the start of the rainy season, is the time when most frogs and toads spawn. The males usually arrive at the ponds first, where they croak to attract females. When a female arrives, a male firmly takes hold of her.

**Below:** Toad eggs are round and black. They absorb the Sun's warmth and develop quickly.

Newly hatched tadpoles cling to the spawn jelly, while their gills and tails grow.

Tadpoles spend nearly all their lives finding food. They become adult toads after about three weeks.

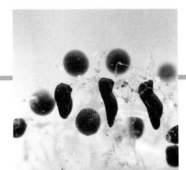

**Left:** The smaller male toad clings to the female as she weaves her egg string around underwater plant stems.

Soon, the female begins to spawn (produce eggs), and the male on her back releases **sperm** into the water to fertilize the eggs. Frogs usually produce a mass of round, black eggs in clear jelly. Toads deposit similarly round eggs, but the eggs are connected in a long string that the female lays as she weaves her way around water plants.

Frogs and toads lay their eggs in shallow water that is warmed by the early spring sunshine. Because the eggs are dark in color, they quickly absorb heat from the Sun. (White eggs would reflect the Sun's heat.) This rapid warming makes the eggs develop and hatch into tadpoles quickly. With such an early start, the tadpoles have all summer to grow into frogs and toads.

As toad tadpoles mature, their hind legs grow. They are one step closer to adulthood.

With well-developed limbs and a shrinking tail, this young toad is ready to leave the water.

On a damp day, baby toads crawl out of their pond and begin life on land.

# Sounds of Spring

**Top:** A baby jackdaw, just out of the nest, calls to be fed.

**Above:** Splendid wrens in Australia live in groups. Only one of the males is brightly colored. All the wrens in a group help raise the babies.

**Right:** The male wren is a tiny bird with a very loud voice. He sings to warn other birds off his territory.

Spring nights are noisy with the croaking of frogs and toads. Spring days have other special sounds because countless birds all sing at once. Birds can tell when day length starts to increase in early spring. Longer days and shorter nights inspire the birds to break into song. Male birds do most of the vocalizing. Their songs are signals to other males, telling them that the territory is occupied.

Each spring morning, especially if the weather is clear, the bird chorus starts before dawn. Just the faintest glimmer of light in the east is enough to wake up the songsters. First, one bird starts. Then within a few seconds, two, three, and — after a minute or so — dozens of birds are singing. Bird songs start in the east because the Sun rises first in the east. If you are up just before sunrise, you will almost always hear the first bird faintly singing far

to the east. You can then hear the thrilling wave of bird songs that spreads across the land, just ahead of the rising Sun.

Not all bird songs can be considered pleasant. Crows croak, bitterns boom, and grouse make extraordinary gurgling sounds. Some birds do not use their voices at all. Snipes dive through the air, making a whirring sound with their tail feathers. Woodpeckers drum with their beaks on hard, dead wood. All these sounds — including the bird song — are related to the same thing. Birds are signaling to each other because spring is nesting time.

**Above:** An African black korhaan male makes a loud, grating call. He calls at the start of the rainy season and makes spectacular display flights.

**Left:** Goldcrests are even smaller than wrens. Their thin, piercing songs are heard by other goldcrests far away.

**Right:** A European robin gathers moss to build its nest. This bird must keep its nesting place secret, so it makes sure no other birds are watching when it flies there.

**Above, far right:** Great horned owls nest early in spring before the trees leaf out. These owls are so big and intimidating to other birds that they do not need to hide their nests.

**Right:** A male mistle thrush feeds pieces of earthworms to his hungry chicks.

Birds build nests to protect their eggs. Unlike some animals that lay hundreds of eggs, birds lay only a few. Therefore, their eggs are extremely valuable to them. Birds spend a lot of time caring for the eggs and the chicks. Without this care, the chicks would never become adults.

Many birds nest in spring so that when the chicks hatch, there is plenty of food for them. Chicks that come into the world in spring have all summer to feed and grow into strong adults that can hopefully survive the winter.

Mistle thrushes start to nest in *early* spring. They feed their chicks earthworms that live in the

soil throughout the year. The worms stay deep underground in frosty weather, but as soon as the ground thaws, they come to the surface. Adult thrushes find the worms and then know that it is safe to start nesting.

Sparrow hawks eat small birds. They also catch them to feed to their chicks. Sparrow hawks start nesting in *late* spring. They delay nesting until that time because many young birds of other species have just left the nest and are plentiful. Sparrow hawks can easily catch these young birds. They then feed them to their own chicks, which are still in the nest.

**Above:** Red fox cubs or pups are born in early spring. In late spring, they venture forth to explore the world.

**Right:** European rabbits do not breed during the coldest months. When spring comes, the doe makes a warm nest for her babies.

Everywhere in springtime — in woods, ponds, meadows, lakes, and seashores — animals produce babies. Red foxes give birth to litters of three or four smoky cubs or pups in underground dens. Badger cubs are also born underground in early spring. By the time these youngsters are old enough to leave their dens, grass and other plants have flourished. The vegetation hides the animals from danger. In spring, there are plenty of grasshoppers and other creatures for the cubs to eat. Spring is a good time for animals to be born.

Increasing light and warmth in spring makes grass grow quickly. **Herbivores**, such as rabbits and voles eat fresh grass. With a plentiful food supply, these animals start to breed. The first litters of

**Left:** Badger cubs are born underground in spring. They do not come out of their burrows, however, until there are plenty of tall grasses and plants to hide them.

rabbits and voles are born in spring. A rich diet of new grass allows the mothers to produce plenty of milk to feed them.

In the vast, arid lands of Australia, kangaroo mothers produce babies any time of year. Often, the babies do not survive because the mothers cannot find enough food for themselves — let alone enough to produce milk for the babies, called joeys. When the rains come, plants grow rapidly. Then, there is enough food for the mothers to produce milk, allowing the joeys to thrive.

The natural world awakens in spring. Plants grow, birds sing, and a multitude of insects appear. Spring is also a time of hard work for animal mothers — and some animal fathers. Eggs need to be cared for. Babies must be looked after and fed. Most of Earth's creatures spend the sunny days of spring having and raising their families.

**Above:** A kangaroo joey comes out of its mother's pouch to explore the fresh green growth of an Australian spring.

# Activities:

## Spring Packages

The first day of spring in the Northern Hemisphere is March 20 or 21, but the first signs of spring appear much earlier. In some areas, catkins lengthen, and early flowers open before mid-January. The farther away from the poles, the earlier the spring. Nearer the poles, temperatures are lower, more snow falls, and winter lasts longer. Spring also arrives late in mountainous districts, where the winters are cold. Just as the dawn chorus of bird songs sweeps across the land each morning from east to west, the greening and flowering of the land sweeps from south to north each spring — or from north to south in the Southern Hemisphere.

### An Early Spring

By bringing a little bit of the outside world indoors, you can make some signs of spring appear early. The extra warmth inside is like several weeks of spring weather outside. Catkins will quickly respond by lengthening and producing pollen. Tree buds will swell, and leaves and flowers will open.

Do the following experiment to produce an early glimpse of spring. You will need water, some vases, a magnifying glass, a needle, pruning shears, and a hammer (*bottom, left column*). On a cold day in early spring, cut a selection of budding twigs from different species of trees. Some species will last longer than others, so try many different kinds. Make sure each twig is long. You will need to trim all of them later.

When you return home with the twigs, cut the ends diagonally with the pruning shears, making sure the twigs are all the same length. Lightly hammer the ends of the twigs so that the ends are crushed. Then, stand the twigs in water (with the crushed ends in the water). Crushing the ends of the twigs helps them

take up water. If you don't crush the ends, air might find its way into the very fine tubes that hold sap in the twig. The air would then keep water from getting into the tubes.

The winter buds of trees are tightly wrapped packages that contain tiny folded leaves and flowers. Sap that rises in spring causes the leaves to unfold and burst out of the buds.

To see how the contents of a bud are packaged, lift the scales off a large bud with a needle. Notice how many layers of scales there are. The inner scales of many buds are covered in fine, silvery hairs that help protect the delicate contents of the bud. Inside the bud, you may find little, pale green leaves (*opposite, right column*).

If it is a flower bud, however, you may be able to see the beginnings of flowers. Use a magnifying glass to get a closer look.

## Water Magic

The warmth of springtime gradually raises the temperature of the water in ponds and ditches. As the water becomes warmer, tiny animals start to multiply.

Try this experiment and see for yourself by artificially warming some pond water. You will need a large glass jar and a warm, sunny windowsill in your house or schoolroom to keep it on. Use a magnifying glass to identify some of the animals you find. A microscope would be even better.

Do this experiment in early spring soon after the ice has melted. Ask an adult to help you gather some pond water. The adult should first stir the mud at the bottom of a shallow pond, and then scoop up a jar of the thick, muddy water. Be careful.

The mud will soon settle to the bottom of the jar, which leaves clear water on top (*below, right*). At first, you will see nothing moving in the jar. As the water warms, however, damselfly and mayfly larvae may struggle to the surface of the mud. In a day or two, many small creatures will be visible. Look at them closely with a magnifying glass or microscope.

You may see round, green volvoxes spinning slowly as they drift through the water. Glasslike daphnia and cyclops rapidly move across the jar. Strands of bright green algae will grow visibly from day to day. All these tiny animals and plants spent the winter as

eggs at the bottom of the pond. The warmth of spring on the windowsill started them growing. When you have finished watching your mud creatures grow, ask an adult to carefully put them back in the pond where you found them.

If you live in a region with a warm climate where there are distinct rainy and dry seasons, you can do this same experiment in the dry season. Scrape up some hard-baked mud from the bottom of a dried-up pond. Stir the mud into a jar of water.

Tiny fairy shrimps and many other creatures may soon appear (*above*). The shrimps grow very quickly. They have to because some of the rain puddles in which they live last only a few weeks before the water disappears in the heat of the Sun.

# Glossary

**adapt:** to change to suit various altered circumstances.

**axis:** the line through the middle of an object around which the object turns.

**breed:** to mate for the purpose of bearing offspring.

**brood:** the young of an animal.

**bulbs:** underground structures formed by some plants from tightly packed, swollen leaf bases.

**catkins:** elongated flowers without petals that usually hang down.

**cold-blooded:** having a body temperature that is the same as the environment.

**day length:** the time between sunrise and sunset.

**equinox:** the time of year when the Sun is directly over the Equator, and day and night are of equal length everywhere.

**fertilize:** to cause a male cell to join with a female cell so that seeds can form or an embryo can grow.

**hemisphere:** one half of Earth, divided at the Equator.

**herbivores:** animals that eat only plants.

**hibernation:** a state of inactivity in which most bodily functions slow down.

**latent heat:** warmth that is necessary to melt a solid or to turn a liquid into a vapor.

**microscopic:** the state of being so small to be visible only with a microscope.

**nectar:** the sweet liquid produced by flowers to attract bees, birds, and other animals for pollination.

**phloem:** the inner bark of a plant that carries sugars and other nutrients to the leaves and flowers.

**pollen:** male cells produced by flowers in the form of fine grains, usually yellow in color. Pollen grains fertilize the female parts of the flowers.

**proboscis:** a tubelike structure on the head of some animals that is normally used for feeding.

**pupae:** the (plural) name given to the stage in the development of insects before they become adults.

**sap:** the watery liquid within plants that nourishes them.

**spawning:** a term used to describe the deposit of eggs. A spawning pond is a body of water where eggs are deposited.

**species:** a group of beings with similar characteristics that are of the same type and that mate.

**sperm:** special male cells, usually actively swimming, whose sole task is to fertilize the female egg cells.

**territorial:** having the characteristic of defending the area around one's home.

**ultraviolet rays:** radiation with wavelengths shorter than visible light.

**warm-blooded:** having a constant body temperature independent from the temperature of the environment.

# Plants and Animals

The common names of plants and animals vary from language to language. Their scientific names, based on Greek or Latin words, are the same the world over. Each kind of plant or animal has two scientific names. The first name is called the genus. It starts with a capital letter. The second name is the species name. It starts with a small letter.

alder (*Alnus glutinosa*) — Europe; introduced to North America 14

badger (*Meles meles*) — Europe, northern Asia, Japan 26, 27

beech (*Fagus sylvatica*) — Europe; introduced to North America 12-13

bluebell (*Endymion non-scriptus*) — western Europe 4-5

common toad (*Bufo bufo*) — Europe; similar species worldwide 18, 20, 21

common zebra (*Equus burchelli*) — southern and eastern Africa 10-11

crocus (*Crocus* species) — cultivated worldwide 14

European rabbit (*Oryctolagus cuniculus*) — Europe, North Africa; introduced to Australia, New Zealand 8, 26

game pheasant (*Phasianus colchicus*) — Asia; introduced elsewhere 4-5

glacier lily (*Erythronium grandiflorum*) — western North America 7

gray kangaroo (*Macropus fuliginosus*) — Australia 27

great horned owl (*Bubo virginianus* ) — North America 24

honeybee (*Apis mellifera*) — kept worldwide 14, 16, 17

magnolia (*Magnolia* hybrid) — China; introduced elsewhere 15

mistle thrush (*Turdus viscivorus*) — Europe, northern Africa, Asia 24, 25

painted lady butterfly (*Cynthia cardui*) — worldwide 9

red fox (*Vulpes vulpes* ) — Europe, Asia, North America, Australia 26

sparrow hawk (*Accipiter nisus*) — Europe, northern Africa, Asia 25

stickleback, three-spined (*Gasterosteus aculeatus*) — Europe, North America 18, 19

wren (*Troglodytes troglodytes*) — Europe, northern Africa, Asia, North America 22

# Books to Read

*Bees: Busy Honeymakers. Secrets of the Animal World (series).* Eulalia García (Gareth Stevens)

*Birds. Wonderful World of Animals (series).* Beatrice MacLeod (Gareth Stevens)

*The Kids' Nature Book. Williamson Kids Can!® (series).* Susan Milord (Gareth Stevens)

*The Nature and Science of Flowers. Exploring the Science of Nature (series).* Jane Burton and Kim Taylor (Gareth Stevens)

*Weather. Young Scientist Concepts and Projects (series).* Robin Kerrod (Gareth Stevens)

# Videos and Web Sites

## Videos

*Frogs and Toads.* (Wood Knapp Video)
*How Does Light Travel?* (Encyclopædia Britannica Educational Corporation)
*How Plants Grow.* (MBG Videos)
*Insects.* (TMW Media)
*The Plant World.* (United Learning)
*Weather.* (DK Vision)
*What's In Your Backyard?* (MBG Videos)

## Web Sites

www.seaworld.org/nature_at_risk/nat endang.html
kids.infoplease.lycos.com/ipka/A0769077 .html
exu.ca/
www.windows.umich.edu/
www.discovery.com/
www.nhm.ac.uk/sc/

Some web sites stay current longer than others. For further web sites, use your search engines to locate the following topics: *butterflies, flowers, hibernation, pollination, spring,* and *toads.*

# Index